LOST AND FOUND

THE TITANIC
AND OTHER
Lost Ships

JOHN MALAM

Copyright © QED Publishing, 2011

First published in the UK in 2011
by QED Publishing
A Quarto Group company
226 City Road
London EC1V 2TT

www.qed-publishing.co.uk

Project Editor Carey Scott
Designer Stefan Morris Design
Illustrations The Art Agency and MW
Digital Graphics
Picture Researcher Maria Joannou

Front cover image: The Titanic departing Southampton in April 1912 and on the bottom of the North Atlantic Ocean today.

A catalogue record for this book is available from the British Library.

ISBN 978 1 84835 593 4

Printed in China

The words in **bold** are explained in the Glossary on page 31.

CONTENTS

What is a lost ship?   4

LOST: Luxury liner   6
FOUND: The *Titanic*   8

LOST: Treasure ship   10
FOUND: The *Atocha*   12

LOST: Cargo ship   14
FOUND: The *Geldermalsen*   16

LOST: Civil War submarine   18
FOUND: *H.L. Hunley*   20

LOST: The King's flagship   22
FOUND: The *Mary Rose*   24

LOST: World War II warship   26
FOUND: HMS *Edinburgh*   28

Timeline of discoveries   30
Glossary   31
Index   32

WHAT IS A LOST SHIP?

The seabed is littered with the wrecks of tens of thousands of ships. They are the world's lost ships, and every one of them has a story to tell about a voyage that ended in disaster. However, their stories can only be told after a lost ship is found.

There are many reasons why ships become lost at sea. The weather is the greatest danger of all for sea captains. Storms, giant waves and fog are all weather hazards and have been the cause of many ships plunging to the seabed. Ordinary human error is also a common cause of ships becoming wrecked. Sometimes, sailors steer their ships too close to rocks, icebergs or other ships so that they crash into them. Piracy is a constant threat and often a real danger. And, in wartime, ships can be sunk when they come under attack from enemy fire.

▲ A marine archaeologist points to an object on the seabed while surveying the site of an ancient Roman wreck off the coast of Italy.

▼ This is a reconstruction of the *Uluburun*, a ship wrecked off the coast of Turkey 3300 years ago. Divers spent 10 years recovering its cargo, which included elephant tusks, ostrich eggs and hippopotamus teeth.

When a lost ship is found, the experts – **archaeologists**, **salvage** operators and professional **treasure-hunters** – can begin to recover objects from it and bring them back up into the daylight for everyone to see. In some special cases, even the ship itself is brought ashore and put on display in a museum.

▲ This 19th-century painting shows galleys – ships powered by oarsmen – in battle. Galleys were used as warships from ancient times up to the 1500s, and were frequently wrecked in sea battles.

The Kyrenia ship

The wreck of an ancient Greek merchant ship from around 300 BCE was discovered at the bottom of the Mediterranean Sea, off Kyrenia, Cyprus in 1965. It took two years to excavate the ship's cargo and raise what was left of her wooden hull. Archaeologists worked out that the Kyrenia ship had been sailing between the Greek islands, transporting wine and almonds, in large pottery jars called amphorae, and millstones for grinding wheat and barley.

LOST:
LUXURY LINER

On 10 April 1912, the biggest and most luxurious passenger **steamship** ever built set sail from Southampton, England. The ship's name was the *Titanic*, and her destination was New York, USA. But the liner was a doomed ship – this was to be her first and only voyage.

Location: North Atlantic Ocean
Date: 14 April 1912

▼ These second-class passengers, photographed boarding the *Titanic*, expected to enjoy a standard of luxury that only a first-class ticket would buy on other ocean liners.

On board the ocean **liner** the *Titanic* was a crew of 899, and 1324 passengers. Among those passengers who were travelling first class were many well-known wealthy businessmen. They were on their way home to the United States after visiting Europe. However, most passengers were poor people travelling third class – the cheapest tickets. They were **emigrants** who had dreams of starting new lives in the USA.

It was not to be. On Sunday, 14 April, the *Titanic* received messages from nearby ships warning of icebergs in her path. The *Titanic* sailed on. Then, as midnight approached, a lookout shouted: "Iceberg, right ahead!" The collision could not be avoided, and the liner's starboard (right) side scraped against the ice mountain, splitting open her **hull** below the waterline.

▶ Luggage trunks and passengers boarding the *Titanic* from a ferry boat at Queenstown, Ireland. This was the liner's last stop before she sailed out into the Atlantic Ocean.

An unsinkable ship?

As the *Titanic* was being built, she was described as 'virtually unsinkable' by her shipbuilders, Harland and Wolff. However, by the time the ship was finished, a rumour had spread that the *Titanic* really was unsinkable. But gaps had been left at the top of the liner's **bulkheads**, so the ship was not completely watertight. When water entered the hull it poured through the gaps, and the *Titanic* was doomed.

WHITE STAR LINE.

"OLYMPIC." 45,000 TONS.
AND
"TITANIC." 45,000 TONS.

THE LARGEST STEAMERS IN THE WORLD.

To **NEW YORK,**
From SOUTHAMPTON—CHERBOURG—QUEENSTOWN.
From LIVERPOOL—QUEENSTOWN.

To **BOSTON,**
From LIVERPOOL—QUEENSTOWN.

For Freight and Passage apply to

THOS. COOK & SON, 31, Fargate, SHEFFIELD; 16, Clumber Street and 97, Derby Road, NOTTINGHAM; and Gallowtree Gate, LEICESTER.

Nothing could stop the cold sea from pouring through the rip in the hull, nothing could stop the ship from flooding, nothing could save the *Titanic* from sinking to the bottom of the North Atlantic Ocean. Of the 2223 people who sailed on the *Titanic*, 1517 drowned or died of cold in the icy water. For the 706 survivors, the night of 14 April 1912 was one they would never forget.

▼ As the *Titanic* sank, survivors in the water saw her stern and propellers lifted up high before she plunged down to the seabed.

FOUND:
THE TITANIC

The *Titanic* had sunk about 800 kilometres off the coast of Newfoundland, Canada, and 3.8 kilometres down. The wreck was so deep, and so far from land, that plans to salvage the ship from her watery grave were not realized for a very long time.

Almost 70 years went by before a serious search to find the *Titanic* finally began. In the 1980s, US explorer Jack Grimm made three attempts at finding the wreck but failed. Someone else who dreamed of finding the *Titanic* was Robert Ballard, a US marine geologist (scientist of the seabed). He had spent years exploring the world's oceans with underwater vehicles, and in 1985 he began to scour the North Atlantic seabed, looking for the long-lost liner.

▶ The *Titanic*'s pursers looked after passengers' valuables, storing them inside leather bags such as this one. Inside were someone's keys, gold watch and purse.

From the control room of his ship the *Knorr*, Ballard operated a tiny **submersible** vehicle named *Argo*. Far below the surface, *Argo* travelled around the seabed, filming its surroundings and sending the images back up to the *Knorr's* screens. For five weeks, Ballard stared at the screens. *Argo* found nothing. Then, it filmed a large metal object on the muddy seabed. Ballard studied the pictures, and realized he was looking at a ship's boiler. *Argo* filmed all around the boiler, looking for the ship it had come from – and that's when Ballard saw the unmistakable shape of a ship on his screen. As more came into view, Ballard could see it was the *Titanic*, lost for 73 years but now found.

▼ Part of the deck of the *Titanic*, photographed in 2003, showing the liner's anchor chains.

The Argo

The *Titanic* was found by the *Argo*, **a remotely operated vehicle**, or ROV. It was a long sledge, lowered into the sea by a crane from the surface ship the *Knorr*. As the *Knorr* moved along, it towed the *Argo* behind it, far below near the bottom of the sea. On board the *Argo* were video cameras that sent moving pictures up to the *Knorr*, and powerful headlights that lit up the underwater blackness.

LOST:
TREASURE SHIP

In September 1622, 28 ships set sail from Havana, Cuba. They were heading home to Spain, loaded with gold, silver and precious stones. This was a Spanish **treasure fleet**, laden with valuables taken from the peoples of Central and South America.

Location: Florida Keys, USA
Date: 5 September 1622

Throughout the summer of 1622, the fleet had sailed around the Caribbean Sea, picking up its cargo of treasure. Among the fleet was a two-year-old wooden **galleon**, the *Nuestra Señora de Atocha*. The *Atocha* went to Cartagena, in present-day Colombia, and Portobello, in present-day Panama. At each port she collected a haul of treasure, filling her hold with silver, gold and emeralds brought from across South America. By August, her hold was packed with riches, and she was ready to join the fleet on the long voyage back to Spain.

As the ships left Havana that September, all eyes were on the sky. Every sailor knew that the hurricane season was about to begin, and the last thing they wanted was to be caught in a howling storm.

▼ Two sailors lower a barrel of treasure into the hold of the *Atocha*, while a third man prepares the next load.

But that was exactly what happened. Gale-force winds battered the ships and huge waves washed over their decks. The *Atocha* was blown northwards, and onto a reef. Water poured through her shattered hull. The great ship sank to the bottom, taking 260 people with her, along with 161 gold bars, 901 silver bars, 250,000 silver coins and a large quantity of **emeralds**. When the storm was over, all that could be seen of the *Atocha* was the stump of her mast poking up above the water's surface. Clinging to it with all their strength were five men – the only survivors.

▲ Here, an artist has captured the sinking of a Spanish treasure fleet in 1715, when all the fleet's 11 ships were wrecked in a hurricane near present-day Florida, USA.

Treasure ships

Spain's merchant ships were large, slow-moving vessels – easy prey for pirates and raiders from England, France and The Netherlands. So, for safety the merchant ships always travelled together in large fleets, and were escorted by warships known as galleons. Although she carried treasure too, the *Atocha* was an escort galleon, and she was armed with 20 cannons. It was her job to protect the other ships of the treasure fleet from pirates.

FOUND:
THE ATOCHA

The treasure ship the *Atocha* sank in 1622. With her mast poking up above the waves, a Spanish salvage team had no problem finding her. Soon after she was lost, divers – holding their breath – went down to the wreck.

The divers could work for only a few minutes at a time until they had to swim back to the surface for air. Try as they might, they could not open the ship's cargo hatches, and the gold, silver and emeralds remained out of reach. So the salvage team brought in pearl divers, who were trained to hold their breath longer than anyone under water. But, by the time they arrived, a second hurricane had ripped the ship's mast off, and now the divers could not find the wreck. After a few months of searching, the team abandoned the operation.

◄ This magnificent cross, made from gold and emeralds, was found inside a silver jewel box on the wreck of the *Atocha*. The back of the cross is decorated with religious engravings.

Pieces-of-eight

The *Atocha* was loaded with 250,000 silver coins, stored inside chests and barrels. These coins were known as pieces-of-eight, a nickname often used to describe old Spanish silver coins. The nickname became used because each coin, or piece, had the same value as eight less valuable coins, called reales. Pieces-of-eight were made in Mexico, Peru, Colombia and Bolivia, for use in Spain.

For the next 350 years, the *Atocha* was at the mercy of the sea. Shifting sands washed over the wreck, her timbers broke up and her precious cargo spilled out over the seabed, only to be buried under a blanket of sand. Then, in the 1970s, US treasure-hunter Mel Fisher began to search for the wreck. It took him years, but in 1985 he at last found ship's timbers on the seabed. They came from the hull of the *Atocha*, and among them Fisher found 130,000 silver coins, 115 gold bars and 315 emeralds, together with bars of silver, and gold chains and coins. This was only the beginning, and over the next few years the *Atocha* gave up more of her secrets. Fisher became a millionaire, and the *Atocha* became one of the richest shipwrecks ever found.

▶ A diver with objects recovered from the wreck of the *Atocha*. He is holding a plate made from pewter – a soft metal made from a mixture of tin and lead.

LOST:
CARGO SHIP

For 200 years, the ships of the Dutch East India Company transported pepper, spices, tea, tropical hardwood and other exotic goods from Asia to Europe. Many of them were attacked by pirates or wrecked by storms, taking their crews and precious cargoes to the bottom of the sea.

Location: Off Bintan Island, South China Sea
Date: 3 January 1752

In 1748, the *Geldermalsen* sailed from The Netherlands, bound for India, Java and China. For two years she sailed around the South China Sea, transporting goods between these countries. Then, in 1751, she sailed to Canton (present-day Guangzhou), on the south coast of China, where she was loaded with cargo to take back to Europe. Into her great hold, packed safely inside wooden crates, went hundreds of tonnes of tea, 147 bars of gold, silks, spices, delicately decorated containers and almost a quarter of a million pieces of fragile Chinese **porcelain** – teacups, saucers, jugs, plates, dishes, bowls and teapots.

▼ This 19th-century painting shows small boats ferrying goods to and from an East Indiaman ship, which looks much like the *Geldermalsen*.

14

Chinese porcelain

In the 1700s, Chinese craftspeople produced a fine white pottery called porcelain, which they hand-painted. It was of a much higher quality than European pottery, and was considered the height of luxury by wealthy Europeans. Chinese potters produced millions of pieces of porcelain for transportation to Europe, where it was sold at high prices.

The *Geldermalsen* began the long journey home in December 1751. It was full of risks. Pirates were a menace, and storms were a constant threat. But the *Geldermalsen* fell victim to a more routine danger – human error. On 3 January 1752, the ship's captain took the wrong course and steered the ship close to a reef, off the island of Bintan, Indonesia. The ship crashed on to the rocks and, as the waves pounded her hull, she broke up and sank. Eighty of the 112 people on board drowned. Her valuable cargo went down with her, and the *Geldermalsen* entered the record books as one of the hundreds of **merchant ships** lost at sea.

▼ In Canton harbour, Chinese workers pack porcelain into wooden crates ready to be stored inside the hold of the *Geldermalsen*.

FOUND:
THE GELDERMALSEN

The *Geldermalsen* sank in the South China Sea in 1752. As she broke up on the seabed, her cargo crates shifted around. Over the years, they split open and rotted away, and their contents fell out. But something else happened as well.

The tonnes of tea the ship was carrying soon spilled from its crates, and the tea leaves floated down onto the thousands of pieces of fragile porcelain. They formed a soft blanket all around the precious pots. Tucked up inside this protective layer of tea, the pots were safe from breaking. They stayed this way until 1985, when the wreck of the *Geldermalsen* was finally found by treasure-hunter Mike Hatcher.

▶ The fine, hand-painted Chinese porcelain that Hatcher recovered from the *Geldermalsen* was as good as new. The dishes, cups and saucers were finally ready to be sold – 233 years later than planned.

Mike Hatcher

An orphan, Mike Hatcher grew up in a children's home in England. When he was 14, he was sent to live in Australia. There he learned to sail and dive, and eventually he became a marine salvor – someone who recovers the cargo from shipwrecks. In 1985 he found the *Geldermalsen* and, in 1999, he located the *Tek Sing* – a Chinese junk that sank in 1822. He is shown here with a sample of the pottery he recovered from that wreck.

It was the find of a lifetime for Hatcher. He located the wreck lying in 40 metres of water off the island of Bintan, Indonesia. The wreck was identified as the *Geldermalsen*, and from it Hatcher raised 170,000 pieces of porcelain, 126 gold bars, the ship's bell, and personal objects that belonged to the crew and passengers. However, it was the porcelain that grabbed people's attention. In 1986 the *Geldermalsen* porcelain was taken to Amsterdam, Holland – its original destination. There it was sold by auctioneer Christie's to wealthy collectors all over the world.

FACT FILE

An estimated 32,500 cups and saucers and 21 gold bars are still on board the *Geldermalsen*.

LOST:
CIVIL WAR SUBMARINE

For four years, from 1861 to 1865, the United States fought a bitter **civil war**. As often happens in wars, new weapons and machines were invented. A submarine was first used in warfare during the American Civil War.

Location: Off Charleston, South Carolina, USA
Date: 17 February 1864

The submarine was called *H.L. Hunley*, after its designer and captain, Horace L. Hunley. She was a true submersible, able to dive and travel underwater, then return to the surface. The *Hunley* was 12 metres long, and was crewed by eight brave submariners. Seven of them turned a handle that made the propeller spin round and the eighth man steered the submarine. But there were problems from the start. While the *Hunley* was being tested, she sank twice, and submariners drowned. But after each sinking she was raised and made ready again.

▼ Artist Conrad Chapman made this painting of the *Hunley* in 1863, when the submarine was in the dockyard at Charleston, South Carolina.

▼ This artist's impression shows the *Hunley* on her mission to sink the *Housatonic*. She carries a single torpedo, mounted at the end of a long spar or rod, which was designed to stab into the wooden hull of the enemy ship.

On 17 February 1864, the *Hunley* went on her one and only mission – to sink the *USS Housatonic*. She was armed with a **torpedo**, carried at the end of a long rod at the front of the submarine. It was packed with about 45 kilograms of gunpowder. The crew fixed the torpedo to the *Housatonic's* hull, then detonated it by pulling a cord – from a safe distance. The torpedo exploded, sinking the *Housatonic* as planned. It was the first time a submarine had been used to sink an enemy ship. But something went terribly wrong, and the *Hunley* sank too, taking the crew with her. This time, the submarine was left on the seabed.

Ironclads

The American Civil War also saw the arrival of 'ironclads'. These were steam-powered ships built of iron – the world's first modern battleships. They signalled the end of wooden warships driven by wind and sail. This is the *Atlanta*, an ironclad that fought on both sides of the Civil War. She began life as a steamship, but was converted to an ironclad of the Confederate States Navy. She was captured by the United States Navy and then fought on their side. Her days ended in 1869, when she was lost at sea.

FOUND:
H.L. HUNLEY

The *H.L. Hunley* was lost in 1864, and for more than 100 years no one knew where the wreck of the little submarine was. Then, in 1970, Edward Lee Spence dived into the murky waters off Charleston, USA, and found more than he was expecting.

Spence was on a fishing trip, and he plunged into the cold water to free a trapped line. He followed the line down. As he tugged at it, he saw it was snagged on something manmade. It was a long, smooth metal object. Spence knew about the Hunley submarine, and as he broke the surface he called out: "I've found the *Hunley*!"

▼ At a conservation centre in Charleston, the *Hunley* was put inside a tank filled with very cold water which stopped micro-organisms from damaging her. Part of the hull was removed, allowing archaeologists to work inside the submarine.

Twenty-five years later, in 1995, divers from the United States'
National Underwater and Marine Agency mounted an
expedition to raise the *Hunley*. After being underwater
for so long, the submarine was partially covered by a
thick layer of sand. Underwater vacuum cleaners carefully
sucked the sand away, and little by little the *Hunley*
was uncovered. To everyone's relief she was in good
condition. The big day finally came on 8 August 2000,
when the lost submarine was gently raised back up to the
surface after 136 years on the bottom. On board were the
remains of her crew – the eight brave men who had lost
their lives way back in 1864. They were buried in 2004,
in Charleston. And the *Hunley*? The submarine is also in
Charleston, where it will eventually go on display in a museum.

FACT FILE

The *Hunley* sank in only
about 3.2 metres of water,
just beyond the entrance to
Charleston Harbour, USA.

◀ This leather purse
belonged to one
of the crew of the
Hunley. It is one
of many personal
belongings found
on board the
submarine by marine
archaeologists.

Lucky gold coin

Among the submariners' possessions that the salvage
team found inside the submarine was a $20 gold
coin. This had belonged to the *Hunley*'s commander,
Lieutenant George E. Dixon. Earlier in the Civil
War, he had fought in the Battle of Shiloh, and
the coin had saved his life when a bullet had
bounced off it. For a lucky charm, Dixon had had
the coin engraved with the words 'Shiloh April
6th 1862 My life Preserver G.E.D.' However, it
failed to save his life a second time.

LOST:
THE KING'S FLAGSHIP

On a summer's day in 1545, a simple mistake caused a Tudor warship to sink close to the English shore. She could have been quickly forgotten, but she was a special ship. Her name was the *Mary Rose*, and she was King Henry VIII's flagship.

Location: Off Portsmouth, England
Date: 19 July 1545

The *Mary Rose* was the pride of the English fleet. She was armed with 91 guns and had a crew of about 415 men. She had fought in sea battles against France – England's old enemy – and was about to do so again. In 1545, France sent an **armada** of 200 ships across the English Channel. They carried an invasion force of 30,000 French soldiers.

▼ The *Mary Rose* was one of the 58 ships of King Henry VIII's navy. As an official record for the king, each ship was illustrated, and its size, crew, armament and basic equipment were described.

King Henry VIII

Henry VIII is one of England's best-known monarchs. He belonged to the Tudor dynasty – a group of strong rulers who made England into a powerful nation. Henry ruled for 38 years (from 1509 to 1547) and is most famous for having six wives, and for changing England from a Catholic to a Protestant country. He was also responsible for building a powerful navy, to which the *Mary Rose* belonged.

Henry VIII ordered a defence fleet to meet the French armada. On the evening of 19 July, as the French ships approached the English coast, the *Mary Rose* led the English fleet of about 80 ships out of Portsmouth harbour. Standing on the shore was King Henry VIII, who could only watch helplessly as the disaster unfolded. The *Mary Rose* had just fired its guns on one side at an enemy ship when it was caught by a strong gust of wind. As her sails filled, the *Mary Rose* leaned over, the open **gunports** dipped below the surface of the sea, and water rushed in. The further over she leaned, the more she filled up. Nothing could be done to stop the *Mary Rose* from capsizing, and down she went, taking about 400 men to a watery grave.

▼ Horrified sailors try desperately to save themselves from drowning in the torrent of water gushing onto the deck of the *Mary Rose.*

23

FOUND:
THE MARY ROSE

FACT FILE

Only the right (starboard) side of the *Mary Rose* has survived. The left (port) side has rotted away.

The *Mary Rose* was lost about one-and-a-half kilometres from Portsmouth harbour. Soon after she sank in 1545, an attempt was made to lift her, but all that was raised were some cannons. The warship was abandoned, and her location was forgotten.

Time passed, and the Tudor warship sank deep into the muddy seabed. Shipworms ate their way through her oak timbers, and powerful sea currents pushed and pulled at her, breaking her open. Then, in 1836, fishermen complained that their nets were getting snagged on a wreck. Two local divers went to investigate. They pulled up some large guns and other items, and experts soon worked out that these came from the *Mary Rose*. But, when the divers stopped working on the wreck, its location soon became forgotten again.

▲ These gold coins are known as 'angels' because they show St Michael with angel's wings, spearing a dragon. Twenty-seven of these 'angels' were found on the *Mary Rose*.

▲ Thousands of ordinary objects were found on the *Mary Rose*, revealing the everyday lives of English Tudor sailors. This set of wooden knives (right) would have had lots of uses, while the fine bone comb (left) was designed for combing out nits.

For the next 135 years, the *Mary Rose* remained at the mercy of the sea and ships passing over her as they sailed to and from Portsmouth. Then, in 1971, an amateur diver, Alexander McKee, found the *Mary Rose* once more. A team of marine archaeologists spent the next 11 years uncovering the 'Tudor time capsule' McKee had found. They recovered almost 20,000 objects from the wreck, and the bones of hundreds of sailors who had drowned in the tragedy. In 1982, the *Mary Rose* herself was carefully raised. She was taken to Portsmouth, the port she had left 437 years earlier, where she went on display in a museum built specially for her.

▼ The hull of the *Mary Rose*, held inside a metal cradle, was raised from the seabed by a giant crane. As the cradle was lifted clear of the water, part of it collapsed onto the *Mary Rose* – but luckily the ship was not damaged.

Preserving the Mary Rose

After so long under water, the timbers of the *Mary Rose* were waterlogged. If they dried out, they would shrink and crack. For 12 years, from 1982 to 1994, she was sprayed with chilled water. This kept her damp. For the following 10 years, from 1994 to 2004, she was sprayed with a waxy chemical called polyethylene glycol (PEG). It soaked into the wood, squeezing the water out and replacing it with wax. This is how the *Mary Rose* has been preserved.

LOST:

WORLD WAR II WARSHIP

On 28 April 1942, 13 merchant ships sailed from Murmansk, Russia. They were heading to Britain, and their journey was full of danger. It was World War II (1939–45), and merchant ships that followed this route were likely to be attacked by German submarines.

Location: Barents Sea
Date: 30 April 1942

Merchant ships that crossed dangerous seas sailed in fleets known as **convoys**. They were protected by escort ships – warships whose job was to fight off attackers and escort the fleet safely home. HMS *Edinburgh* was an escort ship that sailed with the convoy from Murmansk. She was a new ship, launched only four years earlier, and was heavily armed with guns and torpedoes. She was built for battle, but on this voyage the *Edinburgh* also carried a valuable cargo.

Shortly before the *Edinburgh* left Murmansk, 93 wooden boxes were loaded into her bomb room, the safest and strongest room on the ship. The boxes contained 465 bars of Russian gold, weighing five tons and valued at about one-and-a-half million British pounds. The gold was a payment by the Russian leader Joseph Stalin for supplies from Britain.

▼ Briitish sailors load crates packed with gold bars inside the bomb room of HMS *Edinburgh*. The bomb room also contained crates of ammunition.

German U-boat

German submarines are known as U-boats, from the German word *unterseeboot* which means 'submarine'. Germany had more than 1100 U-boats during World War II. The U-456 – the U-boat that attacked HMS *Edinburgh* – was launched in June 1941. She went on 11 patrols, sank six ships and damaged two others. She was sunk in 1943 in the North Atlantic, after being hit by a torpedo dropped from a British plane. Her crew of 49 was all lost.

Two days into the homeward voyage, a pair of torpedoes from a German submarine slammed into the side of the warship. The badly damaged *Edinburgh* tried to return to Murmansk but she was attacked again. In the gunfire, around 60 of the crew were killed. The rest abandoned ship, and the *Edinburgh* slipped below the waves, sinking 245 metres to the bottom of the icy Barents Sea. She took the Russian gold with her, and because it sunk at such a great depth, no one ever expected to see it again.

▲ HMS *Edinburgh* was a British light cruiser warship, armed with twelve six-inch guns and six torpedoes. She had a crew of 750. Before her final voyage, she carried out escort duties, laid mines and took part in the search for the German battleship the *Scharnhorst*.

FOUND:
HMS EDINBURGH

HMS *Edinburgh* sank to the bottom of the Barents Sea in 1942, and her story could have ended there. But her cargo of Russian gold made her different from other World War II wrecks – it was just too valuable to be left on the seabed.

As the years passed, the steel hull of the British warship was attacked by rust, but gold does not tarnish, and the gold bars stored inside her bomb room stayed as shiny as the day they were made. The only change to the gold was what it was worth – it became ever more valuable. By 1980 it was worth an incredible £45 ($64) million, and people were starting to wonder if it could be recovered. One of them was Keith Jessop, an Englishman who owned a company that salvaged shipwrecks.

▼ Bankers, responsible for insuring the gold, thank the organizers of the salvage expedition. In 1981, each bar was worth about £105,000 ($148,000).

▼ Jessop's divers used specialized cutting equipment to penerate the bomb room. Several divers were injured during the long and difficult operation.

Recovering the gold

Because around 60 men had died on the HMS *Edinburgh*, it was designated a 'war grave', which meant it could not be damaged. The British government gave Keith Jessop permission to recover the gold from HMS *Edinburgh* because he promised that his divers would not damage the wreck. Other, bigger salvage companies had asked to recover the gold, but they wanted to blast the wreck open with explosives, which would have destroyed part of the ship.

The British government gave Jessop permission to search for HMS *Edinburgh*. If he found the gold, he could keep 45 per cent as his reward. The rest would be split between the British and Russian governments. In 1981, Jessop found the *Edinburgh*. Divers cut through the armour-plated hull, and after two weeks they reached the bomb room. Of the 465 bars of Russian gold, Jessop found 431 and he became a rich man. A further 29 bars were fished up in 1986. Five bars have never been found, and they are still to this day on board the wreck of HMS *Edinburgh*.

TIMELINE
OF DISCOVERIES

1965
The *Kyrenia* ship, an ancient Greek cargo vessel from around 300 BCE, is found off the coast of Kyrenia, Cyprus.

1971
An English warship, the *Mary Rose*, lost in 1545, is found off the south coast of England. She was raised to the surface in 1982.

1981
HMS *Edinburgh*, a British warship lost in 1942 with a cargo of Russian gold bars, is found in the Barents Sea.

1982
One of the world's oldest shipwrecks, the *Uluburun*, is found off the coast of Turkey.

1984
Pirate ship the *Whydah Gally* is found off Cape Cod, USA. She was lost in a storm in 1717.

1985
The wreck of the *Titanic* is located in the deep waters of the North Atlantic Ocean, where she sank in 1912.

1985
A Spanish treasure ship, the *Atocha*, lost in 1622, is found in shallow water off the Florida Keys, USA.

1985
The *Geldermalsen*, a Dutch merchant ship loaded with Chinese porcelain, is found off the island of Bintan, Indonesia. She was lost in 1752.

1989
The *Bismarck*, a famous German warship of World War II, is found in the Atlantic Ocean.

1995
The *H.L. Hunley*, a submarine lost in 1864 during the American Civil War, is found off the coast of Charleston, South Carolina, USA.

1999
The *Tek Sing*, a Chinese junk carrying 1600 passengers and a cargo of porcelain, is found in the South China Sea. The *Tek Sing* was lost in 1822. She becomes known as 'China's *Titanic*'.

2008
HMS *Victory*, a British warship lost in 1744 off the coast of France, is found.

2010
The world's oldest bottles of champagne and beer are found on a ship wrecked off the coast of Finland 200 years ago. Experts believe they are still drinkable.

GLOSSARY

archaeologist
A person who digs up and studies the remains of the past.

armada
A Spanish word for a fleet of ships.

bulkhead
A dividing wall in the hull of a ship, often creating a watertight compartment.

civil war
A war between people of the same country.

convoy
A group of ships travelling together under the protection of escort ships.

emerald
A bright-green precious stone.

emigrant
A person who leaves his or her own country to start a new life in another place.

galleon
A large, slow-moving and heavily armed ship designed to carry cargo.

gunport
A hole in the hull of a ship through which a cannon is fired.

hull
Main body part of a ship.

liner
Large passenger-carrying ship that sails along fixed routes ('lines').

merchant ship
A ship that transports cargo.

porcelain
A hard, white pottery with a glossy surface. Also known as china.

remotely operated vehicle
An underwater vehicle, or submersible, that is operated from a ship on the surface. It is usually called an ROV.

salvage
Rescue of a wrecked or damaged ship and its cargo.

steamship
A ship powered by steam.

submersible
A small craft that operates under water, usually at great depths.

torpedo
A weapon that travels under water and explodes on impact.

treasure fleet
Ships carrying treasure that sail together.

treasure-hunter
A person who searches for treasure. Some treasure-hunters damage ancient sites and break the law in their search for treasure (looters). Others work with archaeologists.

U-boat (*unterseeboot*)
A submarine of the German navy.

INDEX

American Civil War 18–19, 21
'angels' 24
Argo 9
armada 22, 31
Atlanta 19

Ballard, Robert 8–9
Bismarck 30
bulkheads 7, 31

cargoes 4, 5, 10, 12, 13, 14,
    16, 26
champagne and beer 30
coins 11, 12, 13, 21, 24
convoys 26, 31

dangers 4
Dixon, George E. 21
Dutch East India Company 14

Edinburgh 26–29, 30
emigrants 6, 31

Fisher, Mel 13
fog 4

galleons 10, 11, 31
galleys 5
Geldermalsen 14–17, 30
gold and silver 10, 11, 12, 13,
    14, 17, 26, 28, 29
Grimm, Jack 8
gunports 23, 31

Hatcher, Mike 16–17
Henry VIII 22, 23

H.L. Hunley 18–21, 30
Housatonic 19
hull 5, 6, 7, 11, 13, 15, 19, 20,
    25, 28, 29, 31
human error 4, 15
hurricanes 10–11, 12

icebergs 4, 6
ironclads 19

Jessop, Keith 28–29
jewels 12, 13

Kyrenia ship 5, 30
Knorr 9

liners 6–9, 31

McKee, Alexander 25
marine archaeologists 4, 5, 20,
    25
marine geologists 8
Mary Rose 22–25, 30
merchant ships 5, 11, 14–17,
    26, 31
money chains 13
museum displays 5, 8, 21, 25

Nuestra Señora de Atocha 10–13,
    30

pearl divers 12
personal belongings 8, 17, 21,
    24
pewter 13
pieces-of-eight 12

piracy 4, 11, 14, 15
porcelain 14, 15, 16, 17, 31

reefs 11, 15
remotely operated vehicles
    (ROVs) 9, 31

salvage operators 5, 17, 28–29
Spence, Edward Lee 20
Stalin, Joseph 26
steamships 6, 19, 31
storms 4, 10–11, 14, 15
submarines 18–21, 26, 27
submersibles 9, 18–21, 31
survivors 7, 11

Tek Sing 17, 30
Titanic 6–9, 30
torpedoes 19, 27, 31
treasure fleets 10–11, 31
treasure-hunters 5, 13, 16–17,
    31

U-boats 27, 31
Uluburun 4, 30

Victory 30

war graves 29